NATIONAL GEOGRAPHIC

Ladders

GREAT PLAINS

WHERE ON EARTH?

SEA OF Grass

by Sherri Patoka

This is Scotts Bluff in Nebraska. It is part of the Great Plains. Scotts Bluff was one of the major landmarks that early pioneers saw as they journeyed to the West.

The Great Plains is a vast, mostly flat region of grasslands that lies between the Midwest and the Rocky Mountains. As you stand in the middle of these plains, you notice that the ground is mostly covered with long grasses. This is called a **prairie**. There are almost no trees to block the view of the distant horizon, so the sky seems huge.

When the wind blows across the prairie, the long grasses roll like waves, and it looks almost like you're in the middle of a sea of grass. There are places on the prairie where the grasses are taller than a person.

But not every part of the Great Plains is flat and grassy. As pioneers traveled over the plains to claim land or find adventure in the West, they used a group of buttes called Scotts Bluff (pictured here) to track their progress. A **butte** (BYOOT) is a steep hill with a flat top. It looks like a mountain with its top sliced off. After traveling for weeks on the flat prairies, pioneers were glad to see buttes rising from the plains.

Where on Earth?

THE GREAT PLAINS

As you can tell from this map, the Great Plains region covers parts of ten states in the middle of the United States. There is a lot to see in this land of long grasses gently rolling under a big sky. Let's explore.

Montana

North Dakota

South Dakota

Wyoming

The Oregon Trail

Colorado

New Mexico

Wyoming

Rising more than 1,200 feet from the prairie, Wyoming's Devils Tower was the first national monument in the United States. It's a mass of hard volcanic rock that rose up through Earth's crust millions of years ago. The rock around it wore away, leaving its deeply cracked side and flat top.

Kansas

Prairie dogs have their own towns! They live underground throughout the Great Plains. These little rodents are expert tunnel diggers, and they build each room for a reason. They have sleeping rooms and toilet rooms. They even have rooms in their tunnels where prairie dogs can listen for danger. You can visit them at Prairie Dog State Park in Kansas.

The Oregon Trail

When the United States was still a young country, most of its people lived in the East. People began moving west, seeking land and adventure. The Oregon Trail stretched from the Missouri River to western Oregon. In the 1840s, thousands of people traveled this trail in groups of covered wagons called wagon trains.

Nebraska

Can you imagine giant pigs and small rhinos roaming the middle of the United States? Millions of years ago, different kinds of animals roamed the prairies. There were even beardogs—predators almost as big as wolves! Fossils from the Ashfall Fossil Beds in Nebraska paint a clear picture of what life was like in prehistoric times. These workers are uncovering the fossilized bones of a rhinoceros that lived 10 million years ago.

Nebraska

Kansas

Oklahoma

Texas

Oklahoma

Some pioneers wanted to stay on the Great Plains as they moved west. But without trees for wood, they needed different kinds of materials to build their homes. The answer was sod, the thick prairie surface soil held together by grass roots. Only a few sod houses remain today. You can see them at the Sod House Museum in Oklahoma.

Check In What words can you use to describe the Great Plains?

From Field to

by Cynthia Clampitt

Farming is important on the Great Plains. You can see why when you look at these Kansas wheat fields. The gold areas in this photo are all wheat fields ready for harvest.

Table

If you were in a low-flying plane traveling across the Great Plains, what would you see? The land below you would look like a checkerboard. Each square is a farm growing a different crop. There might be a few brown patches on the checkerboard where the farmers haven't planted yet. That is **topsoil**, the nutrient-rich top layer of soil in which plants grow. The topsoil of the Great Plains is some of the deepest and richest in the world. Plenty of sunshine and an underground water supply make this land perfect for farming.

The Great Plains region has been called the nation's breadbasket because so much of the United States' wheat crop is grown here. Wheat is ground into flour, which is then used to make bread and many other foods. But wheat isn't the only food grown here. Corn, soybeans, sugar beets, and many other crops thrive on the Great Plains.

In spring, farmers plow the fields and plant the crops. Summer sun and rain help the crops grow and ripen. Late summer and autumn is the time for harvesting, or picking the crops. Great Plains' farmers help to feed people all over the United States and Canada—and the world!

Bring on the Machines

When American explorer Zebulon Pike went to check out the country's western lands in the early 1800s, he claimed that the prairies were impossible to farm. The sod, or the grasses and their roots, formed a tough layer that couldn't be broken up for planting, and there wasn't enough water. Too bad he couldn't see beneath the surface to the huge source of underground water, which would make growing crops easier. And too bad he hadn't met John Deere.

In 1837, a blacksmith named John Deere invented a steel plow that could "bust" through the sod. The farmers who used it became known as **sodbusters**.

Things have changed a lot for farmers since the days of John Deere. The hard work of farming has become easier and faster with bigger and better equipment. Farming the land still takes a lot of time and energy, but today's monster machines sure make the job easier—and a little more fun.

Farmers work on huge tractors that weigh 20 tons, which is the weight of about 10 cars! These tractors have tires taller than the height of a grown man.

> Huge machines such as this combine (KOM-byn) make the farmer's job easier. A combine cuts the wheat, separates the grain from the rest of the plant, and cleans it. One machine does it all.

The Big Three

The Great Plains farmers grow lots of different crops, but there are three crops that are most commonly grown on the Great Plains. The "big three" are corn, wheat, and soybeans. They go from tiny seeds to plants in the field to food on your table, all in one growing season.

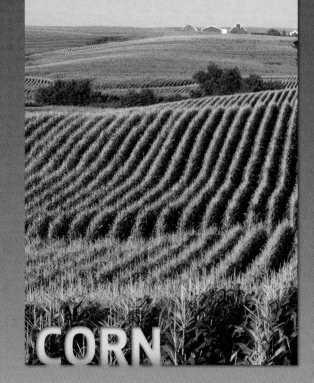

CORN

More American farmers grow corn than any other crop. The Great Plains state of Iowa grows more corn than any other state. A typical Iowa corn plant can grow to be eight feet tall.

You may have eaten corn on the cob before. Did you know that corn can be boiled down to make a sweet syrup?

∧ Corn is used in many foods, like these taco shells. Corn is also used to make fuel for cars, a sweetener for toothpaste, and ingredients in paint, vitamins, and even spark plugs!

WHEAT

Individual grains that grow on stems of wheat are called kernels. There are about 50 kernels on one stem.

The wheat your pizza dough is made with was originally brought to the Americas by European settlers. It was an easy crop to grow.

∧ Wheat is ground into flour and used to make cereals and baked goods such as bread. We eat only the grains. The stalks are used in straw for animal bedding—and in making paper.

SOYBEANS

Have you ever eaten *edamame* (eh-duh-MAH-may)? *Edamame* is the Japanese word for soybean.

Farmers change where they plant their crops every few years. Replacing corn or wheat fields with soybeans some years is a good idea. Soybeans add soil nutrients that those other crops need to grow.

∧ Toasted soybeans make a tasty snack. Soybeans can be turned into soymilk and used in granola bars. Soybeans can even be used to make ink.

Follow the Farmer

The Great Plains gets busy at harvest time. Farmers like John start their day before sunrise. They have few breaks, working from sunup to sundown and later, seven days a week. Let's take a look at some of the things John does during the day when the wheat is ready to harvest.

8:00 A.M. I like to make sure I'm really comfortable when I climb into my combine. That's because I spend most of the day sitting in this machine. It got its name because it combines so many tasks, from cutting the wheat and separating it from the stalks to removing the husks that surround the grains.

SUNRISE After feeding the cows and pigs, I grab the day's eggs from the henhouse. I take a few of the eggs into the kitchen and eat a big breakfast. I usually look over my fields when the sun comes up to judge what needs to be done. Today, the wheat looks ready for harvesting.

NOON Sometimes things go wrong. Machine parts break, or, like today, the combine gets clogged up. When that happens, I have to fix the problem right then and there. Winter is coming, and the crops must be harvested. I don't have any time to lose. After making the repairs, I relax in the shade while I eat the two sandwiches I packed for lunch.

4:00 P.M. It's time for me to pump some of the grain into a waiting truck. I like to have the truck follow the combine into the field, so the combine never has far to go once it's full. When the grain is loaded, I will haul it to a storage facility where it will dry out and keep until I'm ready to sell on market day.

9:00 P.M. It's dark now, but I'm still at work. I want to finish up this section of my wheat fields. Combines have many lights on them because we farmers often work long into the night, especially during harvest. After this load of grain is moved to the truck, I'll eat a late dinner—then relax and spend time with my kids before getting to bed. Tomorrow's another busy day!

Check In What makes the Great Plains so good for farming?

Read to find out about how farm families struggled to survive during the Dust Bowl.

THE DUST BOWL

by Becky Manfredini

> "O BEAUTIFUL FOR SPACIOUS SKIES,
> FOR AMBER WAVES OF GRAIN,
> FOR PURPLE MOUNTAIN MAJESTIES,
> ABOVE THE FRUITED PLAIN!"
>
> —FROM "AMERICA THE BEAUTIFUL,"
> BY KATHARINE LEE BATES

In the early days of settling the Great Plains, this broad land truly was filled with "amber waves of grain." The area became so popular for farming that by the end of the 1920s, farmers had planted millions of acres of wheat on the Great Plains. In fact, they planted so much wheat that they overused the land, plowing and planting it too regularly. Constantly planting the same crop made the soil weak, but the worst was yet to come.

Just a few years later, a horrible **drought**, or period with little or no rain, hit the region. Farmers' crops withered and died before their eyes. Vast fields of wheat were destroyed, and even worse, the dried-out topsoil no longer had plants holding it in place. High winds picked up the loose soil and whirled it away in dust storms.

In 1935, newspaper reporters nicknamed the area suffering from the drought and dust storms the **Dust Bowl**. It included parts of Colorado, Kansas, Texas, Oklahoma, and New Mexico. Soon "Dust Bowl" became a popular term to describe the time of the dust storms themselves as well as the area of the Great Plains where the storms took place.

Dark clouds of dirt blew hard and fast through small towns. They covered homes with a thick layer of dust.

BLACK BLIZZARDS

Imagine you're outside in a blizzard with blowing, swirling snow stinging your face. You can't see anything but white. Now imagine the snow is black—and it's not cold outside. You're in a "black blizzard," the worst kind of dust storm. The people in the Dust Bowl could see a black blizzard coming: a huge wall of black dirt in the distance, quickly rolling in, a huge cloud of grime swallowing up the sun's rays, and then . . . darkness.

The worst black blizzard happened on April 14, 1935. This account is from an article in the *New Republic* magazine. It was written by Avis D. Carlson, who lived through the storm.

The impact is like a shovelful of fine sand flung against the face. People caught in their own yards grope for the doorstep. Cars come to a standstill, for no light in the world can penetrate that swirling murk. . . . We live with the dust, eat it, sleep with it, watch it strip us of possessions and the hope of possessions.

Richard Sell from Perryton, Texas, wrote this about the same day:

Our mother . . . came running out of the house. She was frightened. She told us to get into the house immediately. . . . I looked to the northwest and saw a terrible, solid wall of rolling darkness approaching. Within minutes everything was dark, and the wind and dust were coming into the house everywhere. . . . That terrifying day is as clear in my mind as though it happened last year.

> The most powerful dust storms could carry millions of tons of soil across the Great Plains. The wind swept up the soil from farmland and scattered it far away.

A massive dust storm approached the town of Elkhart, Kansas, in 1937. The only safe place was behind closed doors once the storm reached the town.

It was dangerous to breathe the dust whipped up by a black blizzard. It was also very hard to escape it if you had to go outdoors.

AFTER THE DUST SETTLED

After about eight years of drought and dust, the dust storms finally ended. But the suffering continued. Homes were ruined and the crops had failed. With no crops to sell, many families couldn't pay their banks what they owed them for their land. The banks took back the land, and many families lost their farms.

Penniless and desperate, thousands of families headed west to California to escape the dust. As **migrant workers**, they traveled from farm to farm in search of steady work. They often followed the seasons, moving from place to place as crops were ready for harvesting.

Along country roads of the Great Plains in the 1930s, you could see people leaving their homes and most of their belongings behind. They crammed what they could fit into their trucks or cars and drove away. Many people who lost their farms were too poor to own cars, so they hopped on moving trains that were headed to places where they might find work.

People everywhere were looking for jobs—but there weren't any. The government helped by starting programs like the Civilian Conservation Corps (CCC) that gave people jobs. The CCC workers planted rows of trees on the Great Plains to protect the soil from wind erosion. Farmers were encouraged to leave some fields unplowed for a while, letting nutrients build up and natural grasses grow to keep the soil in place. The Dust Bowl had taught farmers how to take better care of the land.

In 1939, the rains finally came, ending the long drought. Once more, golden waves of wheat grew on the Great Plains.

This boy was careful to cover his nose and mouth during a dust storm.

∧ Winds deposited loose soil in large drifts on this Kansas farm.

∧ This farm family headed west. They hoped to find a better life there.

Check In What challenges did people face trying to survive on the Great Plains during the Dust Bowl?

Neither Rain nor Sleet...

NOR OUTLAWS

by Jeff Osier

This painting by Frank McCarthy
shows a Pony Express rider.
He is on his long ride between
St. Joseph and Sacramento.

They galloped nearly 2,000 miles over the Great Plains and across the rugged western mountains, from Missouri to California. They rode through territory claimed by Native Americans who were determined to defend their homelands. They faced thunderstorms and even blizzards. They were tough, light enough not to weigh a horse down, and unafraid of danger. These brave riders carried mail for the Pony Express. An **express** is any kind of system that delivers goods or messages at high speed.

An advertisement for the Pony Express

More and more people were moving to California in the 1850s. The goal of the Pony Express was to provide a reliable mail service between this new state and the rest of the country. Up until then, ships carried most of the mail to and from California, sailing all the way around the southern tip of South America each way. That could take a month or longer.

The Pony Express came to the rescue. Across land, the route might be dangerous, but it promised to be fast. The goal was to deliver mail from St. Joseph, Missouri, to Sacramento, California, in only 10 days using relay stations. A **relay** is the passing of something from one person to another. There were more than 150 stations along the Pony Express route. A rider would ride from one station to the next. There, he would exchange his exhausted horse for a fresh one. After exchanging horses at several stations, the rider would hand off the mail pouch to another rider, who would carry the pouch on the next leg of its journey.

SIERRA NEVADA

GREAT BASIN

Sacramento

Carson City

Salt Lake City

DELIVERING THE GOODS

Pony Express saddles had built-in pouches. The pouches held mail, money, and news. The news that Abraham Lincoln had been elected president in 1860 was one of the most important Pony Express deliveries.

Casper

Chimney Rock

Devil's Gate

Salt Lake City

Cheyenne

Pony Express riders faced dangers and **harsh**, or very rough, conditions every day. A rider like Johnny Fry (pictured below) might have described his day at work like this . . .

The Pony Express oath says no swearing, no being unkind to the horses, and no fighting. But there was nothing in the oath saying I couldn't be scared!

Three days ago, robbers attacked the Pony Express station at Rock Creek. They stole some of the horses and wounded poor Reynolds, who was tending the station while I was riding like mad toward Rock Creek!

I wasn't very far from the station when I heard the gunshot. I couldn't tell what direction it came from or even how close it was, so I just kept riding. When I got to Rock Creek, the robbers had just escaped, and the local doc was tending to Reynolds and his gunshot wound. I was shaken up, but I traded my worn-out horse for a fresh one and hit the trail again, keeping my eye out for bandits.

I made it to the next two stations before dark, and boy, was I glad to get to the end of my route in one piece. Now I'm beat and ready to sleep. But that gunshot I heard just before Rock Creek is still on my mind. Reynolds is lucky—he's going to be all right— but I sure hope I don't tangle with any robbers myself. No one's lost a mail pouch on this route yet, and I don't plan on being the first!

> No one is sure who rode the very first leg of the Pony Express route. Most people think it was Johnny Fry. On April 3, 1860, he set out from St. Joseph, Missouri. He was carrying the first pouch of mail to be delivered to Sacramento, California.

As speedy as it was, the Pony Express only lasted 18 months. Why did this service end? Blame it on the telegraph, a way of sending messages over long distances through electrical wires. On October 24, 1861, telegraph wires finally connected the East Coast of the United States to the West Coast, carrying messages from New York to California in a matter of minutes rather than days. That was the end of the Pony Express, but it lives on in the legends of the Great Plains and the Wild West.

Fairbury

St. Joseph

Marysville

Check In What problem did the Pony Express solve?

WILD WEATHER

by Becky Manfredini

Welcome to Tornado Alley

Take cover—it's a twister! If you've watched the movie *The Wizard of Oz*, you probably remember Dorothy, her dog Toto, and their farmhouse. They were sucked up into a violent whirl of wind called a **tornado**. Although that story is fictional, tornadoes can really cause terrible damage. A tornado can rip off roofs, uproot trees, and destroy anything in its path. Part of the Great Plains region is called Tornado Alley because tornadoes tear through frequently without much warning.

The area known as Tornado Alley is actually bigger than we thought. The "new" Tornado Alley has grown as our global climate has changed.

What causes a tornado? During a severe thunderstorm, warm, moist air near the ground rises quickly into the colder clouds above. The warm air cools, and its moisture falls as strong rain and large hail. Meanwhile, air rushes in from all directions to fill the space the warm air left below. This air starts whirling around fiercely, and a funnel-shaped cloud forms. If the funnel cloud dips down all the way to the ground, it becomes a tornado. The inside of a tornado can suck up anything in its path. Though a tornado can last from only a few seconds to a few hours, most twisters last about 10 minutes, which can feel like an eternity.

Many of the 1,000 tornadoes that strike in the United States each year happen in Tornado Alley in late spring or early fall. This tornado touched down on the plains of southeastern Colorado near the town of Campo.

Look at this whopper! Huge hailstones like this one can drop from the sky before a tornado.

Tornado Tracking

We know how tornadoes form and where they strike most often. But how can we tell if one is headed our way? Scientists called **meteorologists** study and predict weather. Meteorologists are the people on TV, the radio, and the Internet who warn us when bad weather is headed our way. They pay close attention to the temperature, wind speed, and moving air masses. They watch carefully for conditions that could lead to severe weather such as tornadoes. They are weather watchers and tornado trackers!

Doppler radar is a meteorologist's secret weapon. It sends out long, invisible radio waves. The radio waves hit clouds and **precipitation**, or water falling from the sky, and bounce back to the radar system. That gives meteorologists a picture of how dangerous a storm is and how fast it is moving.

^ The Doppler radar tower at a National Weather Service Station

Doppler radar can identify tornadoes. You've probably seen Doppler radar on TV or on a smartphone. Doppler maps are color-coded by how much rain is falling. They can show a storm moving across the screen, too.

Twisters can destroy entire neighborhoods—even towns—in an instant. Every second counts when it comes to warning people so they can seek cover. Meteorologists issue two levels of alerts when a tornado might be coming. They issue a "tornado watch" when weather conditions could lead to a tornado. They issue a "tornado warning" when a tornado has been spotted. These weather messages help communities stay alert during watches and take cover during warnings, keeping more people safe during tornado season.

Light rain

Heavy rain

> A weather app on a smartphone can keep you alerted to dangerous weather.

Meet a Storm Chaser

It's essential to take cover during tornadoes, but National Geographic Explorer Tim Samaras didn't always do that. Tim bravely raced toward them! He was a storm chaser. His job was to track down tornadoes to study them. He was also an electronics engineer. Tim designed new and improved weather probes. These were small measurement devices that he placed in a tornado's path. Some of the probes contained high-speed cameras that recorded video footage right inside the tornado. Probes help scientists like Tim understand how a tornado forms and determine how dangerous a particular tornado is.

Periscope

Tim Samaras aims his van toward an approaching tornado.

TIM SAMARAS was the lead storm researcher for TWISTEX or the Tactical Weather Instrumented Sampling in or near Tornadoes Experiment. He used science, technology, engineering, and math skills to research tornadoes. Tim hoped that by better understanding tornadoes, he could make more accurate tornado predictions and help people prepare for when a tornado strikes.

As a tornado approached, Tim's probes would get sucked into the center of the funnel. Once there, they measured the temperature, wind speed, humidity, and air pressure in the lower part of the tornado.

From a safe distance, Tim analyzed the data from the probes using laptop computers set up in his van. The van was a weather station on wheels. A domed television antenna on the van's roof allowed him to watch satellite images, weather channel broadcasts, and global positioning system (GPS) readouts that tracked exactly where a storm was. Tim could even view lightning bolts and other amazing weather conditions through a periscope attached to the van's roof.

As a severe storms researcher, Tim Samaras frequently was in dangerous situations in order to make new discoveries about tornadoes. Sadly, Tim, his son Paul, and his research partner, Carl Young, were killed by a tornado on May 31, 2013, as they were collecting scientific data. Tim believed that if he could learn more, then maybe he could help improve our tornado early warning systems.

Severe Weather Pop Quiz

Brilliant lightning flashes across a darkened sky. Thunderclaps boom. Hailstones smash the roofs of cars, and in the distance, a twisting funnel cloud grows larger and darker. It roars like an approaching train. Suddenly it tears off the roof of a house and yanks a towering tree out of the ground. This is the power of a tornado in action.

Scientists know a lot about tornadoes and other severe weather, but there's a lot still to learn. There's also a lot of wrong information out there. Check out the following quiz to test your knowledge!

TRUE OR FALSE?

Open the windows to keep your house safe when a tornado is coming.

FALSE: A tornado's high winds can damage a house whether the windows are closed or open.

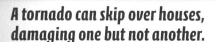

A tornado can skip over houses, damaging one but not another.

TRUE: A tornado may "bounce" up and down at random. You never know where it will land.

Lightning never strikes the same place twice.

FALSE: Lightning is attracted to high, pointed structures. It often strikes them repeatedly.

Tornadoes do not cross water.

FALSE: A tornado over water is called a waterspout.

A basement, closet, or room in the center of a house is the safest place to be during a tornado.

TRUE: And stay away from windows. Windows can break from the force of the wind. Glass will fly!

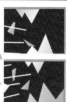

It's a good idea to seek shelter under an overpass or bridge during severe weather.

FALSE: If a tornado forms, it can hit the bridge. You could be hit by flying debris. It's better to find a ditch or ravine and lie facedown in it.

A greenish-looking sky is always a sign of an approaching tornado.

FALSE: A green sky means severe weather. That may or may not include a tornado.

A car can outrun a tornado.

FALSE: A fast-moving car might be able to travel at about 80 miles per hour. But tornadoes can travel that quickly, too. They can also change directions suddenly. And they do not have to stay on the road or wait for traffic.

Check In How do meteorologists and storm chasers use technology to learn about tornadoes?

Discuss

1. What connections can you make among the five selections in this book? How are the selections related?

2. What are some of the challenges and opportunities that are part of living on the Great Plains?

3. How does reading the real-life accounts of people who lived through the black blizzards help you understand what happened during the Dust Bowl?

4. How have the ways that people communicate changed since the time of the Pony Express?

5. What do you still wonder about the Great Plains and the topics discussed in the book?